Today's Superst☆rs
Entertainment

Angelina Jolie

By Jennifer Magid

Gareth Stevens
Publishing

Please visit our web site at www.garethstevens.com.
For a free color catalog describing our list of high-quality books,
call 1-800-542-2595 (USA) or 1-800-387-3178 (Canada). Our fax: 1-877-542-2596

Library of Congress Cataloging-in-Publication Data
Magid, Jennifer.
  Angelina Jolie / by Jennifer Magid.
    p. cm. — (Today's superstars. Entertainment)
  Includes bibliographical references and index.
  ISBN-13: 978-0-8368-9234-5 (lib. bdg.)
  ISBN-10: 0-8368-9234-8 (lib. bdg.)
  1. Jolie, Angelina, 1975—Juvenile literature. 2. Motion picture actors and
actresses—United States—Biography—Juvenile literature. I. Title.
PN2287.J583M34   2008
792.02'8092—dc22 [B]   2008020737

This edition first published in 2009 by
Gareth Stevens Publishing
A Weekly Reader® Company
1 Reader's Digest Road
Pleasantville, NY 10570-7000 USA

Copyright © 2009 by Gareth Stevens, Inc.

Senior Managing Editor: Lisa M. Herrington
Senior Editor: Brian Fitzgerald
Creative Director: Lisa Donovan
Senior Designer: Keith Plechaty
Production Designer: Cynthia Malaran
Photo Researcher: Kim Babbitt

Photo credits: cover Joe Martinez/MPTV; title page, p. 28 Sean Gallup/Getty
Images; p. 5 James Devaney/Getty Images; p. 7 Shkree Sukplang/AFP/Getty
Images; p. 9 Paramount/courtesy Everett Collection; p. 11 Wire Image/Getty
Images; p. 13 Everett Collection; p. 14 AFP/Getty Images; p. 15 Columbia
Pictures/courtesy Getty Images; p. 16 Reuters/Corbis; p. 18 Paramount Pictures/
courtesy Photofest NYC; p. 19 Paramount/courtesy Everett Collection; p. 20
Wire Image/Getty Images; p. 21 AP Images; p. 23 20th Century Fox Film Corp./
courtesy Everett Collection; p. 24 Warner Brothers/courtesy Everett Collection;
p. 26 Sipa Press/Newscom.

Printed in the United States

1 2 3 4 5 6 7 8 9 10 09 08

Contents

Words in the glossary appear in **bold** type the first time they are used in the text.

Chapter 1

World-Famous Mom

In March 2007, Angelina Jolie traveled to Vietnam to adopt a little boy, named Pax. A very private trip quickly became world news. Everywhere she went, Angelina was followed by a group of photographers. This was nothing new for the international superstar. It was a whole new experience for Pax, however. The shy 3-year-old had spent most of his life in an orphanage.

Pax's new mom worried about how all the attention would affect her son. "Photographs and press coverage will make him upset," Angelina said to a Vietnamese newspaper. "I'm very worried about that." Angelina had grown up in the public eye. She knew how difficult that type of life could be.

Wild Child

Angelina's father is Jon Voight, an award-winning actor. Because her father was famous, Angelina was in the spotlight from the time she was a little girl. As Angelina grew up, the public's ideas about her were always changing.

Early in her acting career, Angelina was known as a wild child. She made headlines by doing and saying outrageous things. She won awards for acting. She got more attention for her behavior than for her talent, however.

Fact File

As of 2008, Angelina had been named one of *People* magazine's Most Beautiful People in the World six times.

Angelina Adopts

Angelina has adopted two children in addition to Pax. Her oldest son, Maddox, is from Cambodia. Her oldest daughter, Zahara, is from Ethiopia. The children are from poor countries that Angelina has visited. "Everyone would agree that children need to have a family," she told *People* magazine. "I have the ability to help children fulfill that desire. Why should I say no?"

Zahara (left), Angelina, and Maddox (right) visited Central Park in New York in 2007.

More Than an Actress

Angelina has left her wild ways behind her. She still gets a lot of attention for her personal life, though. Details about her relationship with actor Brad Pitt are always in the news. Even a trip to the park with her kids makes headlines.

As she's gotten older, Angelina has learned how to make the most of all the attention. "I think that when I was in my early 20s, I knew that I wasn't living an important life," Angelina told *Parade* magazine. "I think that I hadn't so much lost my way, but I hadn't found my way. I wasn't giving very much. My life was not really benefiting anyone. That just doesn't feel good."

Giving It Away

Angelina is one of the highest-paid actresses in Hollywood. She makes as much as $20 million per movie. Angelina says that she is overpaid for her acting work. She donates one-third of the money she makes to charity. One-third goes to her living expenses, and she saves the rest.

"I was making a lot of money for something that is a pleasure and realizing how a third of that would end up doing a lot of good," she told *Reader's Digest*. "I just don't need that much. It's a simple decision."

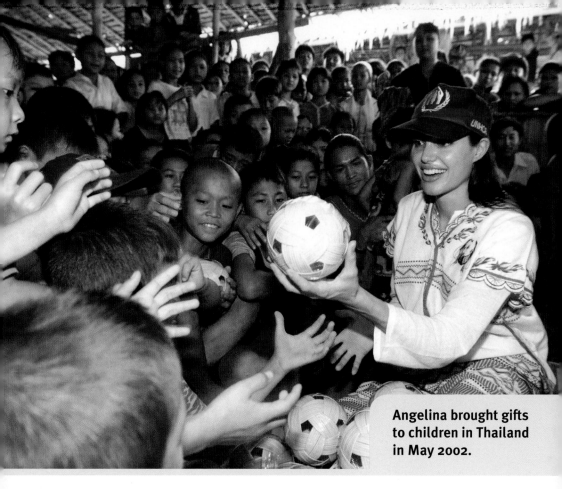

Angelina brought gifts to children in Thailand in May 2002.

A Helping Hand

Angelina now uses her fame to bring attention to less-fortunate people around the world. Being a celebrity has given her a chance to travel. She has seen people suffering from poverty, war, and sickness. She donates her time and money to many charities. Today, Angelina is just as famous for helping others as she is for her acting.

Fact File

In 2004, Angelina started taking flying lessons. She says her dream is to offer her services as a pilot to people in need.

Chapter 2
Acting Out

Angelina Jolie Voight was born on June 4, 1975, in Los Angeles, California. She seemed destined for a career in show business. Her father, Jon Voight, was a popular movie actor. Her mother, Marcheline Bertrand, was a model and an actress.

Angelina's parents divorced when she was just a baby. She and her older brother, James, were raised by their mother. Jon Voight was busy with his acting career. Angelina and James lived in the same city as their father, yet they rarely saw him. "We saw him around Christmastime or at school **recitals**," James told the British newspaper the *Daily Mail*.

Fact File

Angelina wanted to be a funeral director when she was younger.

Angelina got her start in movies at an early age. She appeared in the comedy *Lookin' to Get Out* when she was just 6 years old. The film starred her father, who also cowrote the script.

Still, Angelina says her interest in acting came from her mother. "She loved taking us to the theater," Angelina explains. Marcheline had studied at the famous Lee Strasberg Theater and Film Institute. When Angelina turned 11, she started taking acting classes there, too.

Angelina appeared in the 1982 film *Lookin' to Get Out*. Her real-life father, Jon Voight, played her father in the movie.

Fact File

Angelina is not the only famous student from Beverly Hills High School. Nicolas Cage, David Schwimmer from *Friends*, and Lil' Romeo also attended the school.

Left Out

Angelina and James attended Beverly Hills High School. The school was filled with students who — like Angelina — had famous parents. But there was one big difference between the Voight kids and their classmates. Although Angelina's father was famous, her mother didn't have much money. "We weren't poor," Angelina told *Vogue*. "But because I was the child of an actor, there was an idea that we had a lot of money."

She and James often felt left out. They didn't have the expensive clothes or cars that other students had. The Voights were also picked on at school. Other kids made fun of their second-hand clothing.

Lee Strasberg

Lee Strasberg (1901–1982) was a legendary acting teacher. His students included Al Pacino, Robert DeNiro, and Marilyn Monroe. The Lee Strasberg Theater and Film Institute teaches method acting. This is a form of acting in which actors use their own experiences to make their performances more realistic. For example, to play the part of a person who is sad, an actor might recall how she felt when someone she loved passed away. Angelina has used her method training to give powerful performances in her films.

Famous Father

Over his long career, Jon Voight has appeared in more than 50 movies. He first gained fame for his role as a drifter in the 1969 film *Midnight Cowboy*. By the time Angelina was born, he was one of the most respected actors in Hollywood.

In 1979, Voight won an Oscar for his role as a **paralyzed** war veteran in the movie *Coming Home*. The Oscars are the top film awards. Voight is still active in movies. In 2007, he appeared in *Transformers* and *National Treasure: Book of Secrets*.

Angelina and her brother, James (right), joined their father at the Oscars in 1988.

Never Say Quit

Angelina didn't let problems at school hold her back. When she was 14, she signed with a modeling agency. By the time Angelina finished high school, at age 16, she was going on acting **auditions**. She was rejected almost every time. "I went on a hundred auditions; my mom and I actually checked off the hundredth," she recalled to Backstage.com. Angelina would not let rejection keep her from fulfilling her dreams.

Chapter 3

The Big Break

After Angelina finished high school, her first acting jobs were in music videos. She appeared in videos for the Rolling Stones and Lenny Kravitz, her high school classmate. Angelina also starred in five of her brother's student films.

Angelina was determined to make it in movies. But she was not willing to use her famous last name to get parts. She wanted to win roles because of her talent. Angelina dropped her last name and began using her middle name, Jolie, instead.

In 1993, Angelina landed a starring role in *Cyborg 2*. It was her first big-screen role as an adult. Her character was part human, part machine. Unfortunately, the film was not well received.

Love on the Set

Two years later, Angelina got a leading role in the movie *Hackers*. She played a member of a team of computer geniuses that battle evil. While making the movie, Angelina fell in love with her costar Jonny Lee Miller. The pair got married six months after the film **premiered**.

Hackers got good reviews, and so did Angelina. The movie didn't do much to jump-start her career, however. Angelina appeared in several other movies that didn't get much notice.

In *Hackers*, Jonny Lee Miller and Angelina played rival computer experts.

A Star on the Rise

Angelina's breakout role came in the 1997 television movie *George Wallace.* She played the wife of the real-life Alabama governor who tried to stop **integration** in schools. In 1998, Angelina won a Golden Globe award for her role. The film industry had finally noticed her acting talent.

Golden Again

Just one year later, Angelina was back onstage at the Golden Globes. This time, she accepted the best actress award for her performance in *Gia.* The TV movie told the story of a supermodel whose drug addiction led to her death from AIDS.

Angelina's career was picking up steam. Her personal life was not going as well, though. She and Jonny divorced in 1999. "I'll always love him," she says. "We were simply too young."

Angelina proudly showed off her Golden Globe award for *Gia*.

Oscar Winner

In March 2000, Angelina's star rose even higher. She won an Oscar for her performance in the 1999 film *Girl, Interrupted*. The movie was about young women living in a mental hospital. Winona Ryder was supposed to be the star of the movie. But Angelina's performance as the troubled teen Lisa stole the movie.

Fact File

With her Oscar win, Angelina and her father joined a very small club. The only other father and daughter to win Oscars for acting are Henry and Jane Fonda.

A New Love

A month after her Oscar win, Angelina had another life-changing event. She married actor Billy Bob Thornton. They had met while making the movie *Pushing Tin.*

Their relationship drew a lot of attention. One reason was their age difference. Billy Bob is 20 years older than Angelina. Also, the couple seemed to look for ways to shock people. For example, they each wore a **vial** of the other's blood around their necks! The **tabloids** followed Angelina's every move. Soon, she would start making headlines for very different reasons.

Angelina and Billy Bob Thornton seemed to enjoy all the attention they received.

Chapter 4 — More Than a Pretty Face

Angelina's Oscar win helped her become a major Hollywood star. She started to get offers for bigger roles with bigger paychecks. In June 2000, she starred as a car thief in *Gone in 60 Seconds*. It was her first film to earn more than $100 million.

Next, Angelina starred in *Lara Croft: Tomb Raider*. The film was based on a popular video game. Lara Croft is an adventurer who travels the world. She battles all types of **villains** as she searches for hidden treasures.

Tomb Raider made more than $270 million worldwide. No action film with a woman in the lead role had ever made that much money.

A New Chapter in Life

Tomb Raider was not just a box-office hit. It also took Angelina's life in a new direction. The movie was filmed in Cambodia. Angelina fell in love with the country and the people who lived there. She also saw how poor most Cambodians were.

Filming in Cambodia had a huge effect on Angelina. "I was very focused on myself, on my career, on my life," she told CNN. "We have so much and we want for other things, and we don't realize how grateful we should be." Angelina donated money to build a school in the town where *Tomb Raider* was filmed.

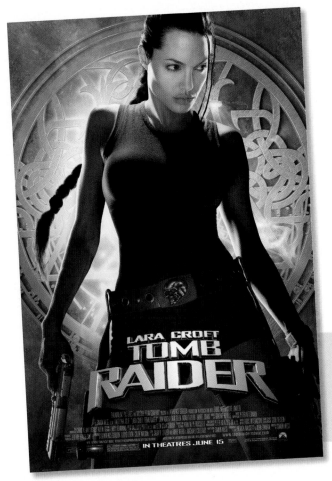

Angelina got good reviews for her first role as an action hero in *Tomb Raider*.

Hello and Good-Bye

Angelina asked her father to appear with her in *Lara Croft: Tomb Raider*. In the film, Jon Voight plays Lara's long-lost father. In real life, Angelina and her dad hadn't been very close. She thought that working together would give them a chance to connect.

In an interview, Angelina said that the experience was "us saying hello and good-bye." Shortly after filming, the two had a falling out. She and her father have not spoken since. Still, Voight is very proud of Angelina. "She's using her celebrity for the good," he told Fox News.

Spreading Goodwill

Research for her role in *Beyond Borders* inspired Angelina to do more for people in need. In the film, she played a woman who worked with the United Nations to help **refugees**. The movie wasn't based on a true story. However, it did show the real-life problems that refugees face. Angelina read everything she could about refugees around the world. Then she contacted the United Nations to see what she could do to help.

In *Beyond Borders*, Angelina played a woman who helped refugees. The role inspired her to do the same in real life.

19

Angelina traveled to countries in Africa on behalf of the Office of the United Nations High Commissioner for Refugees (UNHCR). The UNHCR is dedicated to protecting refugees around the world. In August 2001, the UNHCR invited Angelina to become a goodwill ambassador. She would no longer just be an actress. Her second job would be to visit refugees around the world. She would educate people back home about their struggle.

Maddox smiled for photographers in New York City in May 2003.

Meeting Maddox

In 2002, Angelina returned to Cambodia to film the **sequel** to *Tomb Raider*. While there, she visited an orphanage. She decided to adopt a baby boy. "For me, it makes perfect sense to go to an orphanage and find a child that needs a home," Angelina told *People* magazine. She adopted 7-month-old Maddox in March 2002.

A New Angelina

Her new roles as an ambassador and a mother changed Angelina. She and Billy Bob no longer seemed to have a lot in common. The two divorced a year after Angelina adopted Maddox. We had different ideas about how we wanted to live our lives," Billy Bob told *GQ* magazine in 2004. "She's all over the world, and I respect her for it."

Angelina was busy being a mom. "Becoming a parent changed everything," she told *People*. "My priorities straightened out. My life is all different."

In August 2003, Angelina visited refugees from Chechnya, Russia. A civil war in the region forced thousands of people from their homes.

Fact File

Angelina keeps journals during her travels for the United Nations. In 2003, her journals were published in a book called *Notes from My Travels*.

Chapter 5 One Big, Happy Family

In 2005, yet another film role changed Angelina's life. She costarred in the action-comedy *Mr. & Mrs. Smith* with Brad Pitt. They played a husband and wife who secretly were trained **assassins**.

Critics saw how well Brad and Angelina got along on-screen. Rumors about a real-life romance started to spread. At the time, Brad was married to actress Jennifer Aniston. He and Angelina said that they were just good friends.

Things changed soon after the movie came out. Brad announced that he was divorcing Jennifer Aniston. A month later, photographers caught him and Angelina walking on the beach with Maddox. Their secret was out.

People couldn't stop talking about Brad and Angelina. For the media, it was a match made in heaven. Two of the most popular, most attractive stars in the world were a couple. The tabloids started to call them "Brangelina."

The Jolie-Pitts

In June 2005, Angelina and Brad traveled to Ethiopia in Africa. There Angelina adopted a baby girl, named Zahara. Months later, Brad adopted Maddox and Zahara. The children's last name changed to Jolie-Pitt.

Fact File

In 2004, Angelina voiced a fish named Lola in *Shark Tale*. The movie was nominated for an Oscar for Best Animated Feature.

Brad Pitt and Angelina first got to know each other on the set of *Mr. & Mrs. Smith*.

Brad starred with George Clooney and Julia Roberts in *Ocean's Eleven*.

Brad's Star Power

Brad Pitt is more than just one-half of the most beautiful couple on the planet. He is also one of the top actors in Hollywood. Brad was born in Shawnee, Oklahoma, on December 18, 1963. He studied journalism in college but dropped out to become an actor. A small role in the 1991 film *Thelma & Louise* made him a star.

Brad first caught the public's attention because of his good looks. Like Angelina, he showed that he was more than just a pretty face. In 1996, Brad was nominated for an Oscar for his performance in *12 Monkeys*. His other film credits include *Ocean's Eleven, Seven,* and *Fight Club*.

Brad has also made helping others a big part of his life. In September 2006, he and Angelina started the Jolie-Pitt Foundation. The charity has helped victims of Hurricane Katrina, among other causes.

Meanwhile, Brad and Angelina worked on expanding their family even more. After filming the movie *The Good Shepherd*, Angelina announced she was pregnant.

Welcome, Shiloh

In early 2006, Brad and Angelina traveled to Namibia, Africa. They wanted their baby to be born far away from the American media. The Namibian government banned photographers from taking the stars' pictures. Some photographers were even forced to leave the country!

On March 27, Angelina gave birth to a daughter, Shiloh. Brad and Angelina knew the press would do anything to get photos of their daughter. They wanted to show Shiloh to the world on their own terms. Brad and Angelina sold the first photos of Shiloh for about $4 million. Then they donated the money to **UNICEF**, a United Nations organization that helps children around the world.

Fact File

Angelina's growing family celebrates more holidays than most. "We celebrate Moon Festival for my boys, who are from Asia, and Kwanzaa and things like that," she told *People*. "We certainly try to celebrate as many [holidays] as we can, and celebrate all culture."

A Growing Family

Ten months after Shiloh was born, Angelina and Brad decided to adopt again. That's when Pax joined the family. "Something changed for me with Shiloh," Angelina told *Reader's Digest.* "We had [Maddox] and [Zahara], and neither looked like Mommy or Daddy. Then suddenly somebody in the house looked like Mommy and Daddy. It became clear to us that it might be important to have somebody around who is similar to the other children so they have a connection." In May 2008, Angelina announced she was pregnant again—with twins!

The first official photo of Shiloh Jolie-Pitt appeared on the cover of *People* magazine in June 2006.

A Couple With Heart

Brad and Angelina support many charities. The couple gives a lot because they have a lot to give. But Angelina is quick to point out that anyone can make a difference. She says the Internet, newspapers, and magazines are good tools for researching causes. "I think the first step is to try to navigate your way through some of that and see where your heart goes," she told Parade.com.

Balancing Act

Angelina continues to split her time between her family, her job as a goodwill ambassador, and making movies. In 2007, she starred in *A Mighty Heart.* The film was based on a true story of an American reporter who was kidnapped in Pakistan. Angelina played Marianne Pearl, the reporter's wife. Angelina earned a Golden Globe nomination for the role.

New Challenges

In 2008, Angelina starred in three very different films. *Kung Fu Panda* is an animated family film. Angelina provided the voice of the Master Tigress. In *Wanted,* Angelina once again played a professional killer. She also worked with legendary **director** Clint Eastwood on *Changeling.* In that film, Angelina played a woman whose son has been kidnapped.

Fact File

Angelina and Brad bought a house in New Orleans in 2007. They wanted to show they were committed to helping the city rebuild after Hurricane Katrina.

Counting Her Blessings

Angelina has never been more popular. She has a wonderful family and has used her fame to help countless people. She considers herself to be very lucky. "I am fortunate enough to have a job and go to work and we get to travel and — and do a lot of great things in the world and meet amazing people," she told *Dateline NBC*. "I'm just very fortunate in my life."

Time Line

1975   Angelina Jolie Voight is born on June 4, in Los Angeles, California.

1996   Marries Jonny Lee Miller, her costar in *Hackers*.

1999   Wins a Golden Globe for her role in the TV movie *Gia*; divorces Jonny Lee Miller.

2000   Wins an Oscar for *Girl, Interrupted*; marries Billy Bob Thornton. (They divorce in 2003.)

2001   Stars in *Lara Croft: Tomb Raider*; is named goodwill ambassador for the United Nations.

2002   Adopts her son Maddox while filming *Lara Croft Tomb Raider: The Cradle of Life*.

2005   Stars in *Mr. & Mrs. Smith* with Brad Pitt; adopts her first daughter, Zahara.

2006   Gives birth to her daughter with Brad Pitt, Shiloh, in Namibia, Africa.

2007   Adopts her son Pax; stars in *A Mighty Heart*.

2008   Stars in *Kung Fu Panda*, *Wanted*, and *Changeling*.

# Glossary

assassins — professional killers

auditions — tryouts for roles in movies, plays, or TV shows

critics — in entertainment, people whose job is to give their opinions about movies, TV shows, or music

director — a person who is in charge during the filming of a movie or TV show

integration — bringing people together, regardless of race, color, or religion

paralyzed — unable to move or feel a part of the body

premiered — was shown in public for the first time

recitals — musical performances by singers or dancers

refugees — people who are forced to leave their homelands because of war or persecution

sequel — a film that continues the story of an earlier film

tabloids — newspapers and magazines that focus on stories about celebrities

UNICEF — the United Nations Children's Fund; a part of the United Nations that helps children around the world

vial — a small bottle, usually used to hold liquid

villains — evil characters in movies, plays, TV shows, or video games

To Find Out More

Books

Movie Acting. Making Movies (series). Geoffrey M. Horn
(Gareth Stevens, 2007)

*Notes from My Travels: Visits with Refugees in Africa,
Cambodia, Pakistan, and Ecuador.* Angelina Jolie
(Simon & Schuster, 2003)

DVDs

Hackers (MGM, 1998)*

Lara Croft: Tomb Raider (Paramount, 2001)*

Mr. & Mrs. Smith (20th Century Fox, 2005)*

Shark Tale (DreamWorks Animation, 2005)

*Rated PG-13

Web Site

www.unhcr.org/help/3f94ff664.html
Learn more about Angelina's work for the UNHCR
and find out how you can help.

Index

About the Author

Jennifer Magid is a writer and editor who has worked for MTV, *In Style*, *Teen People*, and Weekly Reader. She has also written for a number of magazines and web sites on everything from health to fashion. Jennifer has lived all over the country, from Oregon to New York. She currently lives in Dallas, Texas, with her dog, Ajax. She dedicates this book to her niece Maddy, who loves reading.